My instaAwesome Life

Written by Kelly Hargrave

Illustrated and designed
by Nancy Panaccione

Tangerine
Press

an imprint of
■ SCHOLASTIC
www.scholastic.com

Copyright ©2015 Scholastic Inc

Scholastic and Tangerine Press and associated logos are
trademarks of Scholastic Inc.

Published by Tangerine Press, an imprint of Scholastic Inc,
557 Broadway, New York, NY 10012
Scholastic Canada Ltd., Markham, Ontario
Scholastic Australia Pty. Ltd, Gosford NSW
Scholastic New Zealand Ltd., Greenmount, Auckland
Grolier International, Inc., Makati City, Philippines
Scholastic UK, Coventry, Warwickshire

10 9 8 7 6 5 4 3 2 1

ISBN: 978-0-545-83987-7

Printed and bound in Jiaxing, China

ENJOY!

Photo Credit: cover top right: Dori OConnell/iStockphoto; cover center right: Sarah Bossert/iStockphoto; cover center bottom left: Lighthaunter/iStockphoto; cover center left: kirin_photo/iStockphoto; cover bottom right: mediaphotos/iStockphoto; cover top center right: budgetstockphoto/iStockphoto; cover center: tvirbickis/iStockphoto; back cover top left: cristianl/iStockphoto; back cover top center: cristalsimon/iStockphoto; back cover top right: Todor Tsvetkov/iStockphoto; 5 bottom left: Pali Rao/iStockphoto; 5 top left: KevinDyer/iStockphoto; 5 center right: ronstik/iStockphoto; 5 center left: jrwasserman/iStockphoto; 6 background: luanateutzi/iStockphoto; 8: pigphoto/iStockphoto; 10 top left: Ben-Schonewille/iStockphoto; 10 top right: Razvan/iStockphoto; 10 bottom: Stockphoto4u/iStockphoto; 11 top center: billnoll/iStockphoto; 11 top left: gmalandra/iStockphoto; 11 center left: penguenstok/iStockphoto; 11 center right: McIninch/iStockphoto; 11 center: cristianl/iStockphoto; 13 bottom: TatyanaGl/iStockphoto; 13 top: AVAVA/iStockphoto; 13 center bottom left: ssuaphoto/iStockphoto; 13 center bottom right: lainea/iStockphoto; 13 center top: trgowanlock/iStockphoto; 26 bottom left: amygdala_imagery/iStockphoto; 26 bottom right: Stephanie Zieber/iStockphoto; 27 bottom left: iVangelos/iStockphoto; 27 top left: telnyawka/iStockphoto; 27 bottom right: AZarubaika/iStockphoto; 27 top right: yuriyzhuravov/iStockphoto; 27 center right: CoffeeAndMilk/iStockphoto; 31 bottom: IS_ImageSource/iStockphoto; 32 top: 4FR/iStockphoto; 41 bottom left: by_nicholas/iStockphoto; 41 top left: Lighthaunter/iStockphoto; 44 bottom: emyerson/iStockphoto; 44 center: Dori OConnell/iStockphoto; 48: poligonchik/iStockphoto; 49 top right: Blacqbook/iStockphoto; 49 center: Heather Dakota; 49 center left: ftwitty/iStockphoto; 49 center right: oculo/iStockphoto; 49 push pins: MrJPEG/iStockphoto; 49 top left: Nancy Panaccione; 52 background: billnoll/iStockphoto; 54 bottom: Lise Gagne/iStockphoto; 55 top: Chiyacat/iStockphoto; 55 center top right: Joe Biafore/iStockphoto; 55 bottom left: Christopher Futcher/iStockphoto; 55 center bottom right: LouieBaxter/iStockphoto; 55 center bottom left: Nuli_k/iStockphoto; 55 center top left: sduben/iStockphoto; 55 bottom right: picalotta/iStockphoto; 57 top right: koi88/iStockphoto; 59 bottom: kinemero/iStockphoto; 59 top: srckomkrit/iStockphoto; 61 top left: PeopleImages/iStockphoto; 62 bottom: Sadeugra/iStockphoto; 62 top: Todor Tsvetkov/iStockphoto; 72 top: Sarah Bossert/iStockphoto; 75: tvirbickis/iStockphoto; 80 right: opreaistock/iStockphoto; 80 center: bernashafo/iStockphoto; 82: wholden/iStockphoto; 83: magnez2/iStockphoto; 85 bottom: bhofack2/iStockphoto; 86 bottom: belchonock/iStockphoto; 88 top: budgetstockphoto/iStockphoto; 89 top: cristalsimon/iStockphoto; 92 center: blackred/iStockphoto.

IT'S AN AWESOME LIFE!

These days unique beauty tips, craft décor, recipes, and style ideas are all over the Internet, blogs, videos, and TV. CREATIVITY IS EVERYWHERE! But where in the world do people find all of these amazing techniques and tips to share? Better yet, how can you find the right tips and projects that work BEST for you? Well, you're in luck—this book will help you get started!

Whether you're coordinating an outfit, painting your nails, planning a party, trying to eat healthy, or decorating your room, this book helps you express your creative style that will be an insta-hit with both you and your friends! This book is exploding with cool tips and ideas to glamorize your everyday life! So take over the projects and ideas and make them your own.

Get your friends and family to join in on the fun, and don't forget to take pictures along the way!

**// (wink, wink, nudge, nudge)

how *to* use this book

1 Skim through the pages and choose a tip or project to focus on.

2 Your kit comes with craft materials to help make some of the idea magic happen for your projects. Incorporate items that can easily be found around the house or at a local thrift store.

3 The instructions are more like guidelines. So if you feel inspired, add a bit of your own flair. Brainstorm how to make a project different or put your own stamp on it. Write down your thoughts—you'll be surprised at what you can come up with when you give a project a little extra creative juice!

4 As you work your way through an idea, take pictures of each step. This will help capture your progress, plus you can share your photos with your friends and family. Not to mention, next time you want to do a similar project, you'll get through it in no time by looking at the insties.

5 The most important picture is your finished project. Check out your mad skills. Now you can inspire others with ideas, tips, new crafts, or recipes!

Don't forget to take that last photo of your final project.

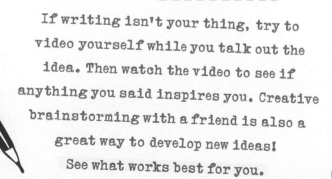

If writing isn't your thing, try to video yourself while you talk out the idea. Then watch the video to see if anything you said inspires you. Creative brainstorming with a friend is also a great way to develop new ideas! See what works best for you.

STUFF IN YOUR KIT

Fabrics in your kit may be different.

Stencil Sheets
Trace onto paper or fabric.

Stickers
Decorate posters, pictures, and other craft projects.

Fabric Scraps
Add to your accessories or clothes.

Yarn
Use the 2 ft. (61 cm) yarn to decorate your clothes and room decor.

Washi Tape
Use for any awesome project you want.

Patterned Paper
The papers can be used for any room decor or party decorating project.